Paul's Letter to the
ROMANS

THE MORNINGSTAR VISION BIBLE

by Rick Joyner

MorningStar Publi

Paul's Letter to the Romans, The MorningStar Vision Bible
by Rick Joyner
Copyright ©2013
Trade Size Edition

Distributed by MorningStar Publications, Inc.,
a division of MorningStar Fellowship Church
375 Star Light Drive, Fort Mill, SC 29715

www.MorningStarMinistries.org
1-800-542-0278

Cover and Layout Design: Kevin Lepp and Kandi Evans

ISBN— 978-1-60708-522-5; 1-60708-522-4

For a free catalog of MorningStar Resources, please call 1-800-542-0278

Paul's Letter to the Romans
TABLE OF CONTENTS

Introduction
Paul's Letter to the Romans

The Epistle to the Romans is widely regarded as the most significant of Paul's letters, and some consider it to be the single most important book in The Bible. It is the clearest explanation of the New Covenant in Scripture. It has also proven to be one of the most powerful books in The Bible, and the single most powerful letter ever written. Just one phrase from it, **"the just shall live by faith," (see Romans 1:17; Habakkuk 2:4)** ignited the Protestant Reformation and changed Western civilization. Certainly the pen in this apostle's hand was more powerful than any sword. No conqueror in history had the impact on the course of civilization than this one letter did.

This letter was written during an important demarcation point in Christian history—the moving of the center of Christian authority, thought, and influence from the Jewish Jerusalem to Rome. This move would lead to some of the best and worst chapters in the Christian story. In this letter to the Romans, Paul accurately forecasted the roots of both.

Luke, a prominent member of Paul's apostolic team, obviously understood the significance of this shift from the Jews to the Gentiles, as it is a main theme of the Book of Acts, which he authored. This shift had more of a theological than geographical significance. It was the departure from Jewish roots and moorings that allowed many heresies to enter and influence the development of Christian doctrine. Some of these led to a terrible darkness and the most evil practices in the history of Western civilization and to this day remain a primary reason why Europe so resolutely resists Christianity.

It took hundreds of years for the church to slide into deep darkness, and it has taken hundreds of years for the church to extricate itself from it. This process still continues as the Reformation is far from complete. This letter to the Romans could have prevented the slide into darkness and has been a primary help for the church to get back on the path of life. It was not heeded for over a thousand years, but when it was rediscovered, the truth in this letter began to turn Christianity back to the life and power of the pure gospel of Jesus Christ.

In Romans, Paul established a strong biblical mooring for the premise that the center of God's message and work had been transferred from the Jews to the Gentiles. Paul wrote that the Jews would be cut off from the advancing purposes of God for a time but would be grafted back in. He explained how the Jews are the "natural branches" and, because of this, would actually be grafted back in much easier when their time came.

In what can now be understood as one of Paul's most important warnings, he exhorted the Gentiles not to become arrogant toward the natural branches, or they also could be cut off. When this warning was neglected, some of the most diabolical doctrines and practices were adopted by institutional Christianity. These led to the persecution of Jews and all Christians who would not embrace the authority of the institutional church. This led to a period of over twelve hundred years of persecution for these groups, which became known by some historians as "the Dark Ages."

Luther, the most prominent of the Reformers and the primary one credited with sparking the Reformation, used the Book of Romans as the main basis of his theology. Even so, he also neglected Paul's warning in Chapters Nine through Eleven to understand the place of Jews according to the flesh and not to become arrogant toward the "natural branches." The rejection of his reformed theology by the Jews embittered him towards them. He also fomented a persecution of the Jews, as well as others, such as the Anabaptists, who would not embrace the whole of his Reformation message. Some of these doctrines and practices

Look

are considered to be the seeds that led to the Holocaust of Jewish people in the twentieth century.

Interestingly, Peter, "the apostle to the Jews," warned about this tragic practice of taking Scripture, or teachings out of context and distorting them. Peter especially warned about those who were doing this with Paul's teachings, as we read in II Peter 3:14-16:

Therefore, beloved, since you look for these things, be diligent to be found by Him in peace, spotless

and blameless, and regard the patience of our Lord to be salvation; just as also our beloved brother Paul, according to the wisdom given him, wrote to you,

as also in all his letters, speaking in them of these things, in which are some things hard to understand, which the untaught and unstable distort, as they do also the rest of the Scriptures, to their own destruction.

One of the great tragedies of Christianity has been the distortion of Scriptures by unstable and untaught people. At times, Paul has been blamed for this bad theology, but those who based their teachings on the writings of Paul distorted what he wrote and taught just as Peter warned against. No doubt Paul's letters and teachings are both sound and insightful. When taken as they were intended, they make the path of life as clear as any of the Scriptures.

I have written over fifty books, and I do not know of one in which the teachings have not been distorted by someone. I speak to an average of two audiences per week, and it is rare for me not to hear people commenting that they heard something very different than what I said, and often the opposite of what I said. Jesus said to "be careful how you hear" (see Mark 4:24), because we are prone to hear what we want to hear rather than what was really said. Since the tower of Babel, mankind has a basic communication problem that is far more serious than just our different languages. This will not likely be corrected until we stop merely listening to words and seek to hear the Word Himself.

The Spirit of Truth requires more than just getting our facts right, though of course we want to do that. Even so, the Spirit of Truth always leads to Jesus, who is the Truth. Truth is a Person, and it is this Person who we must follow. As the Truth Himself made clear in John 7:17:

> **If any man is willing to do His will, he shall know of the teaching, whether it is of God, or whether I speak from Myself.**

The foundation of knowing truth is not just learning proper ex-egesis, but it has more to do with being willing to obey Him. Every truth put forward in Paul's letter to the Romans was in conflict with fallen human nature. To see truth, as it was intended, requires a new heart to understand, and this new heart can only come from a new birth. The demarcation of the center of Christianity from Jerusalem toward the West presented new possibilities to the degree Christians would walk in the new nature. For those who did, and for as long as they did, the power of the New Covenant was greater than any influence the world had ever known.

However, the failure to obey one of the basic commandments to honor our fathers and mothers, which theologically is the Jewish people, opened the gates of hell into the church. Possibly the most important devotion of the Jewish people had been the integrity of the Scriptures and a devotion to obeying them. This devotion was lost within the church for over a thousand years and was replaced by a devotion to a dogma often devised by the most earthly and corrupt of men. It was the rediscovery of the Scriptures as the sole authority for the doctrine of the church that brought about the recovery of truth and life in the church. This began with the recovery of, and devotion to, the Book of Romans.

As Jesus Himself stated, **"The Scripture cannot be broken"
(see John 10:35).** For them to be properly understood, we must
view them as a whole. The Old and New Testaments must be
seen as a whole. All of the references in our New Testament
books to "the Scriptures" are in reference to what we call the
Old Testament. On Paul's first visit to Rome, Luke recorded in Acts
28:23 a message that gives us a very interesting and important
insight into this:

> **When they had set a day for Paul, they came to him
> at his lodging in large numbers; and he was explaining
> to them by solemnly testifying about the kingdom of
> God and trying to persuade them concerning Jesus,
> from both the law of Moses and from the Prophets,
> from morning until evening.**

It is debatable that the authors of the New Testament books,
including Paul, knew that they were writing what would become
canonized Scripture. However, we do know that The Bible of the
first-century church was what we now call the Old Testament.
However, they did not just see it as the law, but as Jesus stated in
Matthew 11:13, **"For all the prophets and the law prophesied
until John."** The first-century church understood how the law
prophesied the coming of Christ in remarkable detail. They used
this to preach the apostolic message—Jesus Christ and the resurrection of the dead.

Paul accurately foresaw that the center of Christian authority
and thought was moving from Jerusalem, and that the world was
entering what Scripture called **"the times of the Gentiles" (see
Luke 21:24).** His letters were intended to prepare the church for
this shift with brilliant and sound teaching, moored resolutely to
the Scriptures. Of his letters, the Book of Romans stands out as the
most comprehensive. Had his message and warnings in this letter
been heeded, Western civilization's history from that time forward

could have been far more brilliant and far less harsh toward the Jews and everyone else.

It is almost universally believed that Romans was written near the close of Paul's third missionary journey. He had just spent nearly three years in Ephesus (see Acts 19:8,10), which would put the writing of this letter between A.D. 55 and A.D. 58 and within twenty-five years of the death and resurrection of Jesus. It was a remarkable and transitional time. This letter was one of the greatest anchors given to Christianity to keep us on the path of life, ever focused on the One who is our life—Jesus Christ.

PAUL'S LETTER TO THE
ROMANS
Romans 1

Apostleship

1 Paul, a servant of Jesus Christ, appointed an apostle, separated for the gospel of God,

2 which He promised before through His prophets in the Holy Scriptures.

3 This gospel is all about His Son, who was born of the seed of David according to the flesh.

4 He was declared to be the Son of God with power, according to the Spirit of holiness, by the resurrection from the dead–Jesus Christ our Lord.

5 It is through Him that we received grace and apostleship to bring to the obedience of faith those from all the nations for His name's sake,

6 among whom you are also called to be in Jesus Christ.

Commendation

7 To all who are in Rome, who are beloved of God, and called to be saints: grace to you and peace from God our Father, and the Lord Jesus Christ.

8 First, I thank my God through Jesus Christ for you, because your faith is proclaimed throughout the whole world.

9 For God is my witness, whom I serve in my spirit through the gospel of His Son, how unceasingly I make mention of you in my prayers

10 making the request that if by any means now, or in time, I may be prospered by the will of God so that I can come to you.

11 For I long to see you in order to impart to you a spiritual gift, which will result in you becoming even more established.

12 I also desire to be comforted by you, and you by me, that we be encouraged by one another's faith.

13 I would not have you ignorant, brethren, that I have often purposed to come to you so that I might have some fruit among you also, even as I do in the rest of the Gentiles, but I was hindered.

14 I am a debtor both to Greeks and to Barbarians, both to the wise and to the foolish.

A Living Faith

15 So, with all that is in me, I am ready to preach the gospel to you also who are in Rome.

16 For I am not ashamed of the gospel—it is the power of God for salvation to everyone who believes, to the Jew first, and also to the Greek.

17 For in this is revealed the righteousness of God from faith to faith as it is written, **"But the righteous shall live by faith" (see Habakkuk 2:4).**

18 For the wrath of God is revealed from heaven against all ungodliness and unrighteousness of men, who hinder the truth in unrighteousness,

19 because that which is revealed about God is manifested in them, for God manifested it to them.

The Roots of Perversion

20 For the invisible things of God have been clearly seen since the creation of the world, being revealed through the things that are made, even His everlasting power and divine nature, so that they are without excuse.

21 It is for this reason that even though they knew of God they did not glorify Him as God, neither did they give thanks, but became vain in their reasoning, and their senseless heart was darkened.

22 Professing to be wise, they became fools,

23 and exchanged the glory of the incorruptible God for the likeness of an image of corruptible man, and even of birds, and four-footed beasts, and creeping things.

24 Therefore God gave them up to pursue the lusts of their hearts, and to debased behavior, so that their bodies should be dishonored.

25 This was because they exchanged the truth of God for a lie, and worshiped and served the creature rather than the Creator, Who is blessed forever. Amen.

26 For this cause God gave them over to the vilest of passions, because their women changed the natural function into that which is against nature,

27 and likewise also the men, leaving the natural function of the woman, burned in their lust toward one another, men with men performing shameful acts, and receiving in themselves the recompense of their error which is due.

28 As they refused to include God in their knowledge, God gave them up to a depraved mind, to do those things that are not proper for man that was created in the image of God;

29 and they became filled with all unrighteousness, wickedness, covetousness, maliciousness, were filled with envy, murder, strife, deceit, and malice. They became slanderers,

30 backbiters, haters of God, insolent, haughty, boastful, inventors of evil things, disobedient to parents,

31 without understanding, covenant-breakers, without natural affection, unmerciful,

32 who, knowing the ordinance of God, and that they who practice such things are worthy of death, not only did they do them, but also encouraged others to practice them.

Apostleship

Romans 1:1-6: Paul was so devoted to the gospel that he could not even write a salutation without sharing it. He also stated the basic truth that the gospel is all about Jesus. Jesus

was then, and still is, the apostolic message. The path of life is not about following directions, but about following the Person of Jesus Christ.

Commendation

1:7-14: The Roman church had become known throughout the world because of its faith. Because of this, Paul wanted to come to them so that he might have some fruit in this great church. There are wellspring churches in every period, and the life that is in them does make others want to be a part of them in some way.

A Living Faith

1:15-19: The Roman church was already known throughout the world for its faith, and in verse seventeen, it is written that the righteousness of God is revealed from faith to faith. This is a progressive, growing faith that we must have if we are to continue in the righteousness of God. Even biology teaches that anything that stops growing has started dying. Is our faith still growing?

The Roots of Perversion

1:20-32: Paul addressed the root of sexual perversion—the darkening of the soul by worshiping the creature and other created things, rather than the Creator. Sexual relations were created by God to be a joy and a blessing to those who worship Him and live the way He created us to live. When sexual deviation or perversion enters into one's life, it is the beginning of a downward spiral into the black hole of self-centeredness and darkness of heart, which the apostle explains here.

In these times, the homosexual agenda and its allies demand the most tolerance, but are themselves the most intolerant of any who disagree with them. The rage that they have toward those who disagree has led to violence and is going in the direction of increasing violence. laws have been passed in some countries forbidding the public reading of Romans Chapter One because of its condemnation of homosexuality. This is a good example of what Paul warned about here.

As Paul wrote in I Corinthians 13:8, "love never fails" or, as it could have been translated, "love never quits." If we love people, we will never abandon the truth that can set them free, regardless of the threats. If we love truth, we will never abandon it, or fail to stand up for it. This is a core reason behind the breakdown of the social order in the last days and will be an increasing point of conflict between light and darkness. Which side will we be on?

NOTES:

PAUL'S LETTER TO THE
ROMANS
Romans 2

Righteous and Unrighteous Judgment

1 Therefore you are without excuse, every one of you who passes judgment on others. In the same way that you judge another, you condemn yourself, if you who judge also practice the same things.

2 We know that the judgment of God is coming to those who practice such things.

3 So consider this, O man, who judges those who practice these things, and yet does the same, do you think that you will escape the judgment of God?

Goodness of God Leads to Repentance

4 Or do you despise the riches of His goodness, and forbearance, and patience, not knowing that it is the goodness of God that leads you to repentance?

5 Your hardness and unrepentant heart will store up for yourself wrath in the day of wrath, which is the revelation of the righteous judgment of God,

6 who will render to every man according to his works.

7 To those who by patience in doing good seek for glory, and honor, and incorruption, they will receive eternal life.

8 To those who are self-seeking and do not obey the truth, but obey unrighteousness, there shall be wrath, indignation,

9 tribulation, and anguish upon every soul of man that works evil, to the Jew first, but also to the Greek.

10 Glory, honor, and peace will be to every man that works good, to the Jew first, and also to the Greek,

11 for there is no respect of persons with God.

The Purpose of The Law

12 As many as have sinned without the law will also perish without the law, and as many as have sinned under the law will be judged by the law.

13 It is not the hearers of the law who are just before God, but the doers of the law will be justified.

14 When Gentiles that do not have the law do by nature the things in the law, these, not having the law, are a law to themselves,

15 as they show the work of the law written in their hearts, their conscience bearing witness with them, and their thoughts either accusing or excusing them.

16 This is for the day when, according to my gospel, God will judge the secrets of men by Jesus Christ.

17 If you bear the name of Jew, and rest upon the law, and glory in God,

18 and know His will, and approve the things that are excellent, being instructed out of the law,

19 and are confident that you yourself are a guide to the blind, a light to those who are in darkness,

20 and able to correct the foolish, a teacher of babes, having in the law the form of knowledge and of the truth;

21 you therefore who teach others, do you not teach yourself? You who preach that a man should not steal, do you steal?

22 You who say that a man should not commit adultery, do you commit adultery? You that abhor idols, do you rob temples?

23 You who glory in the law, through your transgression of the law, you dishonor God.

24 For the name of God is blasphemed among the Gentiles because of you, even as it is written.

25 For circumcision indeed profits one if you are a doer of the law, but if you are a transgressor of the law, your circumcision has become un-circumcision.

26 If therefore the uncircumcised keep the ordinances of the law, shall not his un-circumcision be reckoned as circumcision?

27 Shall not the un-circumcision by nature, if they fulfill the law, judge you, who with the letter of the law, and circumcision, are a transgressor of the law?

The True Jew

28 For he is not a Jew who is one outwardly, neither is circumcision that which is in the flesh,

29 but he is a Jew who is one inwardly, and circumcision is of the heart, in the spirit, not in the letter, whose praise is not from men, but from God.

Righteous and Unrighteous Judgment

Romans 2:1-3: There is a righteous judgment that stands for the truth and righteousness of God, but this becomes hypocrisy and unrighteousness when we practice the same things that we judge others for.

Some use this text to teach that we should not judge anyone. However, this conflicts with other New Testament commandments to judge those who are in the church. Here, it says that we should not judge "if" we are practicing the same things. We must be careful not to take a biblical statement beyond what it actually says. Adding or subtracting from the Word of God is a more serious offense than most other sins.

Goodness of God Leads to Repentance

2:4-11: It is not the fear of judgment that leads to repentance as much as the goodness of God which compels us to love Him, and only love can keep us. This is why the exhortation to "repent for the kingdom of God is at hand" is a call

to repentance, because it is good news, or the gospel of the kingdom, not bad news.

The reason that judgment came to the Jews first was for two reasons: 1) because they had been given the knowledge of sin and righteousness first, and 2) because the Jews were set as the "acid test" for the gospel. They had been hardened, not to condemn them, but for the challenge necessary for the gospel to become what it should be—a message and a life that would make even the most hardened ones jealous for God.

The Purpose of The law

2:12-27: Is it better to have the circumcision in the flesh, but be uncircumcised in heart, or to have a heart that is circumcised but not to have the outward sign? The New Covenant made true religion about the heart.

The True Jew

2:28-29: Is it better to be a Jew according to the flesh, but not worship God, or not to be a Jew but worship Him? The true Jew is the one who worships God in spirit and in truth. Even so, as Paul later asserts in Chapters Nine through Eleven, this does not negate the promises of God to the Jew according to the flesh.

NOTES:

Paul's Letter To The
ROMANS
Romans 3

The Righteousness of God

1 What then is the advantage of being a Jew? Or what does it profit one to be of the circumcision?

2 There is much in every way. First of all, they were entrusted with the oracles of God.

3 So what if some are without faith? Should their lack of faith make the faithfulness of God of none effect?

4 God forbid! Let God be found true, but every man a liar. As it is written, **"That You might be justified in Your words, and might prevail when You come into judgment" (see Psalm 51:4).**

5 But if our unrighteousness demonstrates the righteousness of God, what will we say? Is God then unrighteous when He visits with wrath? (I speak from the reasoning of men.)

6 God forbid! For then how could God judge the world?

7 If the truth of God through my lie abounds to His glory, why am I also still judged as a sinner?

8 Why not (as we are slanderously reported to have said), "Let us do evil, so that good may come?" The condemnation of those who would propose such foolishness is just.

The Unrighteousness of Men

9 What then, are we better than they are? No. Not in any way, because we have before laid to the charge both of Jews and Greeks, that they are all under sin,

10 as it is written, **"There are none righteous, no, not one" (Psalm 14:3).**

11 **"There are none that understand. There are none that seek after God;**

12 **"They have all turned aside, they have altogether become unprofitable. There is none that does good, no, not so much as one" (Psalm 14:2-3):**

13 **"Their throat is an open grave. Their tongues they use for deceit. The poison of asps is under their lips" (Psalm 5:9, 140:3):**

14 **"Whose mouth is full of cursing and bitterness" (Psalm 10:7):**

15 **"Their feet are swift to shed blood;**

16 **"Destruction and misery are in their ways;**

17 **"The way of peace have they not known" (Isaiah 59:7-8):**

18 **"There is no fear of God before their eyes" (Psalm 36:1).**

19 Now we know that what the law says, it speaks to those who are under the law so that every mouth may be stopped, and the whole world may be brought under the judgment of God,

20 because by the works of the law will no flesh be justified in His sight. It is through the law that the knowledge of sin comes.

21 Now apart from the law a righteousness of God has been manifested, which is witnessed by the law and the Prophets,

22 even the righteousness of God through faith in Jesus Christ to all who believe. There is no distinction with God;

23 for all have sinned, and fall short of the glory of God.

The Grace of God

24 We are therefore justified freely by His grace through the redemption that is in Christ Jesus,

25 whom God set forth as a propitiation, so that through faith in His blood shows forth His righteousness because of the forgiving of sins even before they are committed, revealing the unfathomable patience of God,

26 and revealing His righteousness even in this present season. In this way He might Himself be just, and the justifier of those who have faith in Jesus.

27 Where then is the glorying by man? It is excluded. By what manner of law? Of works? No, but by a law of faith.

28 We establish therefore that a man is justified by faith apart from the works of the law.

29 Is God the God of Jews only? Is He not the God of Gentiles also? Yes, of Gentiles also.

30 If it is that God is one, and He will justify the circumcision by faith, and the un-circumcision through faith.

31 Do we then make the law of none effect through faith? God forbid! No, we establish the law.

The Righteousness of God

Romans 3:1-8: God's righteousness can never be nullified by our unrighteousness or our disobedience. Even so, many use the problems that Christians have as an excuse not to believe in God. It is a shallow and foolish argument. God is faithful and true regardless of how much His people fail.

The Unrighteousness of Men

3:9-23: The Jews failed to uphold God's righteousness with lives that reflected it and now so have the Gentiles. Even so, our great and gracious God is willing to extend His grace to both, which He does through the righteousness we can assume through faith in Christ.

The Grace of God

3:24-31: Now that faith in the atoning sacrifice of Jesus is established as the basis of our righteousness, many assume that the law is no longer necessary. As we are told here, it still has a purpose in revealing sin. We must know what sin is in order to know our need for the atonement of the cross. Even so, if we seek to keep the law as our basis of righteousness, we are rejecting the grace extended to us by the cross. Now we seek to obey the law by abiding in Christ

and His righteousness, which is summed up in loving God and loving one another.

NOTES:

PAUL'S LETTER TO THE
ROMANS
Romans 4

Grace by Faith

1 If we establish the law in this way, what then will we say about Abraham, our forefather according to the flesh?

2 Because, if Abraham was justified by works, he has something to glory in, but not toward God.

3 For what does the Scripture say? **"Abraham believed God, and it was reckoned unto him for righteousness" (Genesis 15:6).**

4 Now to the one who works, the reward is not reckoned as from grace, but as a debt owed for the work.

5 However, to the one who does not work, but believes in Him that justifies the ungodly, his faith is reckoned as righteousness.

6 Even as David also pronounced "blessed" the man to whom God reckoned as righteous, which is apart from works,

7 saying, **"Blessed are those whose iniquities are forgiven, and whose sins are covered.**

8 **"Blessed is the man to whom the Lord will not reckon sin" (Psalm 32:1-2).**

9 Is this blessing then pronounced upon the circumcision, or upon the uncircumcised also? For we say, to Abraham his faith was reckoned for righteousness.

10 How then was it reckoned? When he was in circumcision, or in un-circumcision? When he was still un-circumcised.

11 He received the sign of circumcision as a seal of the righteousness of the faith which he had while he was un-circumcised, so that he might be the father of all who believe even when they are un-circumcised, that righteousness might be reckoned to them,

12 and the father of circumcision to them who not only are of the circumcision, but who also walk in the steps of that faith of our father Abraham, which he had while yet un-circumcised.

13 For it was not through the law that the promise came to Abraham, or to his seed, so that he should be heir of the world, but through the righteousness of faith.

14 For if they that are of the law are heirs, faith is made void, and the promise is made of no effect.

15 For the law brings wrath, but where there is no law, neither is there transgression.

16 For this cause it is of faith, so that it may be according to grace, to the end that the promise may be sure to all of the seed, not only to those who are of the law, but also to those who are of the faith of Abraham, who is the father of us all

17 as it is written, **"A father of many nations have I made you" (see Genesis 17:5),** before him whom he believed, (even) God, who gives life to the dead, and calls the things that are not as though they were.

18 In hope Abraham believed when it seemed hopeless, to the end that he might become a father of many nations according to that which had been spoken, **"So shall your seed be" (see Genesis 15:5).**

19 Without his faith weakening he considered his own body then as being as good as dead (he being about 100 years old), as well as the deadness of Sarah's womb (see Genesis17:17, 18:11);

20 yet, looking to the promise of God, he did not waver in unbelief, but grew strong through faith, giving glory to God,

21 being fully assured that what He had promised, He was able also to perform.

22 Therefore it was reckoned to him for righteousness.

23 Now it was not written for his sake alone that it was reckoned to him,

24 but for our sake also, to whom it shall also be reckoned, who believe on Him who raised Jesus our Lord from the dead,

25 Who was delivered up for our trespasses, and was raised for our justification.

Grace by Faith

Romans 4:1-25: The key point of this chapter—that the righteousness of God is imparted by faith to those who have faith in Him—is the fundamental truth of the New Covenant. Being born a Jew had advantages; they had been in a covenant with God and were made custodians of His written Word. However, one must have faith in God and His salvation to be justified. This justification is available to all people.

Being justified by faith does not mean we can disregard the standards of righteousness expressed by the law. Since we cannot keep the law by our own strength, our focus is on abiding in the Lord and trusting His atonement. We must focus on His grace and His power so that we might walk uprightly before Him. In this way, the attention of those who pursue righteousness is on the person of God, on a relationship with Him, instead of on laws.

In verse eighteen, we are told that Abraham believed God even when he thought his situation was hopeless. Anyone can have faith in the difficulties of everyday life, but the greatest faith is demonstrated in the greatest difficulties. True faith in God rises when we face impossibilities. Never waste your opportunities to trust God. True faith is not just believing for an outcome, but trusting God in all things.

NOTES:

PAUL'S LETTER TO THE
ROMANS
Romans 5

We Stand by Grace

1   Therefore, being justified by faith, we have peace with God through our Lord Jesus Christ.

2   Through Him we have had our access by faith into this grace in which we stand, and through Him we rejoice in hope of the glory of God.

The Path to Maturity

3   Not only so, but we also rejoice in our tribulations, knowing that tribulation works steadfastness in us.

4   Steadfastness works godly character, and godly character, hope.

5   This hope will never lead to shame, because the love of God has been shed abroad in our hearts through the Holy Spirit who was given to us.

6   For while we were yet weak, at the proper time Christ died for the ungodly.

7   For one would not die as a propitiation offering for a righteous man, or not even for a good man would one so have to be offered.

8   However, God commends His own great love toward us in that while we were yet sinners Christ died for us.

9   Much more then, being now justified by His blood, shall we be saved from the wrath of God through Him.

10   For if, while we were enemies we were reconciled to God through the death of His Son, much more, having been reconciled, shall we be saved by His life.

11 Not only so, but we also have joy in God through our Lord Jesus Christ, through whom we have now received our reconciliation.

One Atonement for All

12 Therefore, as through one man sin entered into the world, and death through sin, and so death passed to all men, because all sinned.

13 Before the law was given sin was in the world, but sin is not imputed when there is no law.

14 Nevertheless, death reigned from Adam until Moses, even over those who had not sinned after the likeness of Adam's transgression, who is a type of Him who was to come.

15 As is the trespass, so also is the free gift. This is because if it is by the trespass of the one many died, much more did the grace of God, and the gift by the grace of the one man, Jesus Christ, abound to the many.

16 Just as through one that sinned condemnation came, the gift of grace came through One. For the condemnation came through one who sinned, leading to the condemnation of many, and the free gift came through One, leading to the justification of many who had trespassed.

17 For if by the trespass of the one death reigned through the one, much more will they that receive the abundance of grace, and the gift of righteousness, reign in life through the One, Jesus Christ.

18 So then, as through one trespass the condemnation came to all men leading to death, even so through one act of righteousness came justification leading to life for all men.

19 For as through the one man's disobedience the many were made sinners, even so through the obedience of the One will the many be made righteous.

20 So the law came so that the trespass might be made manifest, but where sin abounded, grace did abound even more abundantly.

21 As sin reigned in death, even so might grace reign through righteousness to eternal life through Jesus Christ our Lord.

We Stand by Grace

Romans 5:1-2: The most basic truth that leads to a victorious life is that we stand on the grace of God. His grace is worth much more than a lifetime of effort. It is the impregnable rock that the most stable and effective lives are built upon.

The Path to Maturity

5:3-11: We must keep in mind that trials and tribulations are all for our sake. They prepare us and work in us the characteristics of spiritual maturity. Once we have been tried, the Lord is able to trust us with more of His authority. Then we can be seated with Him on His throne, ruling and reigning with Him in this life. We see here that the progression of maturity is:

1) Steadfastness,

2) Godly character,

3) Hope,

4) The love of God.

The "love of God" is more than just having love for Him—it is also having His love for others. His love enabled Him to make the ultimate sacrifice of His own Son. When we have His love in us, we will no longer live for ourselves but for Him, His people, and His purposes—living the life of the cross as His disciples.

The object of His love was to reconcile the world. When we come to maturity, this ministry of reconciliation will be the drive of our lives—the love of God.

One Atonement for All

5:12-21: Death came through Adam to all men, but life came through Jesus, and it is available to all men by His atonement. There is no other sacrifice for sin but the cross of Jesus. We, therefore, take up our cross, not to gain God's approval, but from a position of having His approval through Christ. The cross of Jesus is enough for all men and all sin, and nothing can ever be added to it or taken away from it. The atonement is complete and finished. Any doctrine that seeks to add to or take away from it is false and is an ultimate blasphemy of this ultimate gift of God.

NOTES:

PAUL'S LETTER TO THE
ROMANS
Romans 6

Deliverance from Sin

1 What will we say then? Should we continue in sin so that grace may abound?

2 God forbid! How can we who died to sin live in sin any longer?

3 Or are you ignorant that all who were baptized into Christ Jesus were baptized into His death?

4 We were buried with Him through baptism into death, so that just as Christ was raised from the dead through the glory of the Father, so we also might walk in newness of life.

5 For if we have become united with Him in the likeness of His death, we will also be in the likeness of His resurrection,

6 knowing that our old man was crucified with Him, so that the body of sin might be done away with, so that we should no longer be in bondage to sin.

7 For he that has died is delivered from sin.

8 If we died with Christ, we believe that we will also live with Him.

9 We know that Christ, being raised from the dead, will die no more. Death has no more dominion over Him.

10 For the death that He died, He died to sin once, but the life that He lives, He lives to God.

11 Even so, reckon yourselves to be dead to sin, but alive to God in Christ Jesus.

The Root of Lawlessness

12 Therefore do not let sin reign in your mortal body, so that you obey its lusts.

13 Neither present your members to sin as instruments of unrighteousness. But present yourselves to God, as one who is alive from the dead, and your members therefore as instruments of righteousness that now exist for God.

14 For sin shall not have dominion over you, for you are not under law, but under grace.

15 Does this mean that we may sin, because we are not under law, but under grace? God forbid!

16 Do you not know that to whom you present yourselves as servants to obey, you belong to the one whom you obey, whether to sin and death, or to obedience and the righteousness that is in life?

17 Thanks be to God that just as you were once the servants of sin, you became obedient from the heart to that form of teaching whereby you were delivered.

18 Being made free from sin, you became servants of righteousness.

19 I speak after the manner of men because of the weakness of your flesh. For just as you presented your members as servants to uncleanness and to iniquity, leading to lawlessness, even so now present your members as servants of righteousness leading to sanctification.

20 For when you were servants of sin, you were free in regard to righteousness.

21 What fruit then had you at that time in the things in which you are now ashamed? For the end of those things is death.

22 However, now being made free from sin, and having become servants of God, you have your fruit leading to sanctification, and the outcome eternal life.

23 For the wages of sin is death, but the free gift of God is eternal life in Christ Jesus our Lord.

Deliverance from Sin

Romans 6:1-11: This is one of the most succinct and clear explanations of our deliverance from sin by the power of the cross. The New Covenant is not just the forgiveness of sin, but deliverance from sin by putting to death our sinful nature. This requires a new birth into a new nature that does not serve sin but righteousness. Through the cross of Jesus, we are not just delivered from the consequences of sin, which is death, but we are also given a new life that is eternal. However, the devil also tries to counterfeit the resurrection we have in Christ by seeking to resurrect our "old man," which is dead. Our old man, or old nature, has died with Christ so that we will no longer have to obey the lusts of the flesh. By abiding in Christ in whom there is no sin, we are now alive and free from sin.

The Root of lawlessness

6:12-23: We are told that impurity and lust lead to lawlessness. Jesus warned that lawlessness would be one of the greatest problems in the last days, and because of lawlessness, the love of many would grow cold. If we give in to impurity or lust, it will cause our love for Christ to grow cold. First, we will become lukewarm, but ultimately, our love for God will grow cold, and we will depart from the faith. We might claim to be believers, yet we will no longer be serving the Lord but rather His enemy. This warning is not to unbelievers, because they do not have love for Him in the first place. The warning is that lawlessness will cause the love of "most" Christians to grow cold. Will we be one of these? We all must choose between our old nature and the new and decide which we will allow to prevail over our lives. One leads to life and the other to death.

NOTES:

PAUL'S LETTER TO THE
ROMANS
Romans 7

The Domain of the Law

1 Do you not know, brethren, (for I speak to men who know the law), that the law has dominion over a man for as long as he lives?

2 For this reason the woman is bound by law to her husband while he lives, but if the husband dies, she is freed from the law in regard to her husband.

3 So then, if while the husband lives she is joined to another man, will she not be an adulteress? But if the husband dies she is free from the law, so that she is not an adulteress, though she is joined in marriage to another man.

4 Therefore, my brethren, you were made dead to the law through the body of Christ, that you should be joined to another, even to Him who was raised from the dead, that we might bring forth fruit unto God.

The Law Exposes Sin

5 For when we were in the flesh, the sinful passions, which were aroused by the law, wrought in our members that which would bring forth the fruit of death.

6 But now we have been freed from the law, having died to that by which we were held, so that we serve in newness of the spirit, and not in the oldness of the letter.

7 What shall we say then? Is the law sin? God forbid. How would I have known sin, except through the law. For example, I would not have known coveting except the law had said, **"You shall not covet" (see Exodus 20:7; Deuteronomy 5:21).**

8 However, sin, finding occasion through the commandment, exposed in me all manner of coveting, for apart from the law sin is dead.

9 I was alive apart from the law, but when the commandment came, sin revived, and I died.

10 For this reason the commandment, which was to lead to life, instead resulted in death,

11 because sin, finding occasion through the commandment, beguiled me, and through it slew me.

12 So the law is holy, and the commandment holy, and righteous, and good.

13 Did that which is good result in death for me? God forbid! But sin, that it might be shown to be sin, by working death in me through that which is good, so that through the commandment sin might be exposed as exceedingly sinful.

14 For we know that the law is spiritual, but I am carnal, in slavery under sin.

15 For that which I do not understand, the very thing that I do not want to do, that I practice. The very thing that I hate, that I do.

16 If I do that which I do not want to do, I agree that the law is good.

17 So it is no longer I that do it, but sin that dwells in me.

18 For I know that in me, that is in my flesh, dwells no good thing. For I desire to do what is good, but the power is not in me to do it.

19 For the good I want to do I am not able to do, but the evil that I do not want to do, I do.

20 If I do that which I do not want to do, it is no longer I who does it, but sin that dwells in me.

21 I find then through the law that to me who wants to do good, evil is present.

22 For I delight in the law of God in my spirit:

23 but I see a different law in my members, warring against the law of my mind, and bringing me into captivity under the law of sin that is in my members.

24 Wretched man that I am! Who will deliver me out of the body of this death?

25 I thank God that I am delivered through Jesus Christ our Lord. So then I, with my mind, serve the law of God, but with the flesh the law of sin.

The Domain of the Law

Romans 7:1-4: Under the law, we are bound in covenant to our first spouse for as long as we both live; this point was to show how we must die to the law, the first covenant, so that we can be joined to Christ. If we are under the New Covenant and still seek to establish our righteousness by the law and continue in a relationship with the law, we are spiritual adulterers.

The Law Exposes Sin

7:5-25: We see the purpose of the law is to reveal sin. For this reason, the law is still useful, not to base our righteousness on how well we keep it, but because it reveals both our sin and our need for the atonement of the cross—the only remedy for sin. Once we have turned to Christ as our remedy, we no longer seek to live by the precepts of the law but to live by the Spirit of Christ who has been given to us.

NOTES:

PAUL'S LETTER TO THE
ROMANS
Romans 8

Deliverance From Condemnation

1   There is therefore no condemnation to those who are in Christ Jesus.

2   For the law of the Spirit of life in Christ Jesus made me free from the law of sin and death.

3   For what the law could not do, because of the weakness of the flesh, God, sending His own Son in the likeness of sinful flesh, and for sin, condemned sin in the flesh,

4   so that the ordinance of the law might be fulfilled in us, who do not walk after the flesh, but after the Spirit.

War Between Flesh and Spirit

5   For those who are living according to the flesh set their minds on the things of the flesh, but those who are living by the Spirit set their minds on the things of the Spirit.

6   For the mind set on the flesh leads to death, but the mind set on the Spirit abides in life and peace,

7   because the mind set on the flesh is at enmity with God, for it is not subject to the law of God, neither indeed can it be.

8   So those who are living by the flesh cannot please God.

9   You are not in the flesh, but in the Spirit, if the Spirit of God dwells in you. If any man does not have the Spirit of Christ, he is not His.

10 If Christ is in you, the body is dead because of sin, but the spirit is alive because of righteousness.

The Victory of the Spirit

11 If the Spirit of Him that raised Jesus from the dead dwells in you, He that raised Christ Jesus from the dead will give life also to your mortal bodies through His Spirit that dwells in you.

12 So then, brethren, we are debtors, not to the flesh, or to live after the flesh:

13 for if you live after the flesh, you must die. If by the Spirit you put to death the deeds of the body, you will live.

The Freedom of the Sons of God

14 As many as are led by the Spirit of God are the sons of God.

15 You did not receive the spirit of bondage leading to fear again, but you received the spirit of adoption, whereby we cry, "Abba, Father."

16 The Spirit Himself bears witness with our spirit, that we are children of God,

17 and if children, then heirs. We are heirs of God, and joint-heirs with Christ, if we suffer with Him so that we may also be glorified with Him.

18 For I know that the sufferings of this present time are not worthy to be compared with the glory that shall be revealed to us.

The Freedom of the Creation

19 For the whole creation waits with great expectation the revealing of the sons of God.

20 For the creation was subjected to futility, not of its own will, but by reason of him who subjected it.

21 This was done with the hope that the creation itself will also be delivered from the bondage of corruption into the liberty of the glory of the children of God.

22 For we know that the whole creation groans and travails in pain together until now.

23 Not only this, but we ourselves also, who have the first-fruits of the Spirit, even we groan within ourselves, waiting for our adoption, and the redemption of our body.

24 For in hope were we saved, but hope that is seen is not hope, for who hopes for that which he already sees?

25 But if we hope for that which we do not see, then we wait with patience for it.

The Helper

26 In like manner the Spirit also helps our weaknesses. Because we do not even know how to pray as we should, so the Spirit Himself makes intercession for us with groaning beyond what can be expressed in human language.

27 He that searches the hearts knows what the mind of the Spirit is, because He makes intercession for the saints according to the will of God.

28 We know that all things work together for good for those who love God, to those who are called according to His purpose.

29 For whom He foreknew He also predestined to be conformed to the image of his Son, so that He might be the firstborn among many brethren.

30 Those whom He predestined He also called, and whom He called He also justified, and whom He justified, those He also glorified.

31 What then will we say to these things except, if God is for us, who could be against us?

The Generosity of God

32 He that did not spare His own Son, but delivered Him up for us all, how will He not also with Him freely give us all things?

33 Who then will lay anything to the charge of God's elect? It is God that justifies.

34 Who is the one that condemns? It is Christ Jesus that died, and was raised from the dead, who is at the right hand of God, who also makes intercession for us.

35 Who will separate us from the love of Christ? Will tribulation, or anguish, or persecution, or famine, or nakedness, or peril, or sword?

36 Even as it is written, **"For Your sake we are killed all the day long. We were accounted as sheep for the slaughter" (Psalm 44:22).**

37 No. In all these things we are more than conquerors through Him that loved us.

38 For I am persuaded that neither death, nor life, nor angels, nor principalities, nor things present, nor things to come, nor powers,

39 nor height, nor depth, nor any other creature, is able to separate us from the love of God that is in Christ Jesus our Lord.

Deliverance from Condemnation

Romans 8:1-4: Even mature Christians often carry a weight of guilt because of their shortfalls, failures, and sins. We do not have to do this. The cross of Jesus is enough for even our worst failures, and it is not for us to try to pay the price for sin that He already paid for on the cross. For this reason, one of the devil's basic strategies against the saints is to get us carrying this guilt so that we do not receive the benefits of the New Covenant. Once we have confessed our sin, we are free from it and must reject the yoke of guilt and condemnation.

War Between Flesh and Spirit

8:5-10: The most desperate battle we all wage is between following the Spirit, the new person into which we have been born again, and the carnal nature, the "old man." One way leads to life and the other to death. We must love God and love life more than we love sin. We must see this battle for what it is—a battle for our lives—and we must resolve to win by following Christ our King.

The Victory of the Spirit

8:11-13: We were given the Spirit to lead us to life, and when we are on the path of life, we will be putting to death the deeds of the flesh. Is there evidence that the carnal nature is being put to death? Are we growing in the fruit of the Spirit? Both of these should be obvious if we are fighting the good fight of faith.

The Freedom of the Sons of God

8:14-18: If we are sons of God, then we will be led by the Spirit of God. When the Spirit is leading our lives, we have the unfathomable satisfaction of a father-son relationship with God. The greatest freedom that we can ever know is that we are known by God, loved by Him, and included in His own family.

The Freedom of the Creation

8:19-25: The corruption, disorder, and bondage in creation were caused by the fall of man. When man fell, all that was under his dominion fell with him. When man takes his place once again in a restored relationship with God, creation will also be brought back into order and the freedom that only this restored order can bring. As the prophets have foretold, this earth will again be the paradise it was originally created to be. This is why the whole creation longs to see the sons of God take their rightful place again in relationship to God. All will be set free when this happens, and the natural state of all of creation is freedom.

The Helper

8:26-31: The Holy Spirit is "the Helper," not the "Doer." He will not do what we are called to do, but He will assist us in all things, even sometimes making the impossible possible if we follow Him.

As we are told here, all things work together for good for those who love God and are called according to His purpose.

The next verse tells us what the good is—that we are conformed to the image of Christ. This is the reason for every trial that we go through—the Lord is working to restore us to His image. This is more valuable than any earthly treasure or any other accomplishment we could have in this life, and it is available to everyone. Knowing this, and letting the Spirit use trials to work His nature into us, is the path of life and peace.

The Generosity of God

8:32-39: We determine the value of any commodity by what someone is willing to pay for it. Consider your value by what the Father was willing to pay for you—the life of His own Son. There could be nothing of greater value in the universe, and that is how much the Father values and loves you. For this reason, there is no power in the universe that can separate us from God and His love.

NOTES:

PAUL'S LETTER TO THE
ROMANS
Romans 9

Grief for Israel

1 I speak the truth in Christ, I do not lie, my conscience bearing witness with me in the Holy Spirit,

2 that I have great sorrow and unceasing grief in my heart.

3 For I would even wish that I myself were accursed, separated from Christ for my brethren's sake, my kinsmen according to the flesh who are Israelites.

4 It is their right for the adoption, the glory, the covenants, the giving of the law, the service of God, and the promises.

5 It is through their fathers that Christ came according to the flesh, who is over all, God, and blessed forever. Amen.

Spiritual Israel

6 However, it is not as though the word of God has been nullified. For they are not all Israel who are of Israel.

7 Just because they are Abraham's seed they are not all children of Abraham, but **"in Isaac shall your seed be called" (see Genesis 21:9-12).**

8 That is, it is not the children of the flesh who are children of God, but the children of the promise are reckoned as His seed.

9 For this is a word of promise, **"According to this season will I come, and Sarah shall have a son" (Genesis 18:7).**

10 Not only this, but Rebecca also having conceived by our father Isaac,

11 and even though the children had not yet been born, neither had done anything good or bad, that the purpose of God according to election might stand, not of works, but of Him that calls,

12 it was said to her, **"The elder shall serve the younger" (see Genesis 25:21-23)**

13 even as it is written, **"Jacob I loved, but Esau I hated" (see Malachi 1:2).**

The Key of Righteousness

14 What shall we say then? Is there unrighteousness with God? God forbid!

15 For He said to Moses, **"I will have mercy on whom I have mercy, and I will have compassion on whom I have compassion" (see Ezekiel 33:19).**

16 So then it is not of him that wills, nor of him that runs, but of God that has mercy.

17 For it was said in the Scripture to Pharaoh, **"For this very purpose did I raise you up, that I might show in you My power, and that My name might be published abroad in all the earth" (see Exodus 9:16).**

18 So then He has mercy on whom He wills, and whom He wills He hardens.

19 You may then say, "Why does He still find fault? For who withstands His will?"

20 No, who are you, O man, who replies in this way to God? Should the thing formed say to Him that formed it, "Why did You make me thus?"

21 Or has not the potter a right over the clay, from the same lump to make one part a vessel for honor, and another for common use?

22 What if God, wanting to show His wrath, and to make His power known, endured with much patience vessels of wrath prepared for destruction,

23 and that He might make known the riches of His glory upon vessels of mercy, which He beforehand prepared for glory,

24 even us, whom He also called, not from the Jews only, but also from the Gentiles?

25 As He said also in Hosea, **"I will call them My people that were not My people; and her 'beloved', who was not beloved"** (Hosea 2:23).

26 **"And it will be, that in the place where it was said to them, 'You are not My people,' they will be called sons of the living God"** (Hosea 1:10).

27 Isaiah cried concerning Israel, **"If the number of the children of Israel were like the sand of the sea, it is but the remnant that will be saved.**

28 **"for the Lord will execute His word upon the earth, finishing it and cutting it short"** (see Isaiah 10:22-23).

29 As Isaiah had said before, **"Except the Lord of Sabbath had left us a seed, we would have become as Sodom, and would have been made like Gomorrah"** (see Isaiah 1:9).

The Key of Faith

30 What will we say then? The Gentiles, who did not seek righteousness, attained righteousness, even the righteousness that is by faith.

31 Israel, following after a law of righteousness, did not succeed at fulfilling the law.

32 Why? Because they did not seek it by faith, but by works. They stumbled over the stone of stumbling.

33 As it is written, **"Behold, I lay in Zion a stone of stumbling and a rock of offence: And he that believes on Him will not be put to shame"** (Isaiah 28:16).

Grief for Israel

Romans 9:1-5: Paul, once "a Pharisee of Pharisees," the most pious religious sect of the Jewish religion and the most devoted patriots of their nation, loved his people and his nation to the degree that he would give up his own salvation for theirs if he could. He wrote this after decades of persecution and threats against his life by the very ones he loved so much. This kind of love could only be God's unconditional love given to Paul for the Jewish people. God proved this unconditional love when He loved them more than He loved His own life and went to the cross on their behalf. To the degree that we walk in these footsteps of Christ and His apostles, we will be ambassadors of His salvation and grace. If we are abiding in Christ, we will also share His love for the Jewish people, who will yet be grafted back into His vine.

Spiritual Israel

9:6-13: Paul loved his brethren according to the flesh, but he also understood that the true Jew was the one who lived by faith in Christ and His atonement. This life of faith in Christ is according to the Spirit, not merely the flesh, which pursues righteousness by works. Jesus also affirmed this when the Pharisees claimed that they were the "sons of Abraham." Jesus countered by telling them that if they were the sons of Abraham, they would do the deeds of Abraham. The true seed of Abraham are those who do the deeds of Abraham, living by faith and seeking the city that God is building, not what is built by man. For Abraham, Isaac, and Jacob, the evidence of their faith and pursuit of God was their contentment to live in tents. They were wealthy and could have built great palaces. However, they were not living for the temporary but for the eternal.

The Key of Righteousness

9:14-29: Paul affirms a basic truth that all who would understand righteousness and justice must comprehend—the Maker of creation is the One who determines righteousness and justice. He can do what He pleases with all He has made. However, what He has been pleased to do is to love us beyond our ability to comprehend. Because of this, He does not only demand justice, but He also extends mercy and grace. We will spend eternity trying to fathom His great love, and even that will not be long enough.

The Key of Faith

9:30-33: The key to faith and walking with God in His purposes is to understand what causes us to stumble—sin—and to also receive the redemption that only comes through Christ. There is no other way to reconcile with the Father except through His Son. We can never compromise this truth if we are to remain on the path of life.

NOTES:

Paul's Letter To The
ROMANS
Romans 10

How Israel Stumbled

1 Brethren, my heart's desire and my supplication to God is for them, that they may be saved.

2 For I bear them witness that they have a zeal for God, but not according to knowledge.

3 For being ignorant of God's righteousness, and seeking to establish their own, they did not subject themselves to the righteousness of God.

Christ is Salvation

4 For Christ is the end of the law for righteousness for everyone that believes.

5 As Moses writes that the man that practices the righteousness that is by the law must live by the law.

6 But the righteousness that is by faith says, **"Say not in your heart, 'Who will ascend into heaven?' (That is, to bring Christ down:)**

7 **"or, 'Who will descend into the abyss?' (That is, to bring Christ up from the dead)"** (see Deuteronomy 30:12-13).

8 But what does it say? **"The word is near to you, in your mouth, and in your heart"** (Deuteronomy 30:14). That is the word of faith that we preach.

9 If you confess with your mouth that Jesus is Lord and believe in your heart that God raised Him from the dead, you will be saved.

10 It is with the heart that man believes, resulting in righteousness; and with the mouth confession is made that leads to salvation.

11 For the Scripture says, **"Whoever believes in Him shall not be put to shame"** (see Psalm 34:22; Isaiah 28:16, 49:23; and Jeremiah 17:7).

Unity in Christ

12 For there is no distinction between Jew and Greek, for the same Lord is Lord of all, and is rich in mercy for all who call upon Him,

13 as it is written, **"Whosoever will call upon the name of the Lord will be saved"** (Joel 2:32).

14 How then will they call on Him in whom they have not believed? How will they believe in Him about whom they have not heard? How will they hear without a preacher?

15 How will they preach, except they be sent? Even as it is written, **"How beautiful are the feet of them that bring glad tidings of good things!"** (Isaiah 52:7)

16 But they did not all heed the good news because Isaiah says, **"Lord, who has believed our report?"** (Isaiah 53:1)

17 So faith comes by hearing, and hearing by the word of Christ.

18 But I say, "Did they not hear?" Yes, for certain they did because, **"Their sound went out into all the earth, and their words to the ends of the earth"** (Psalm 19:4).

19 Did Israel not know? First Moses says, **"I will provoke you to jealousy with that which is not a nation. With a nation void of understanding will I anger you"** (Deuteronomy 32:21).

20 Isaiah is very bold, saying, **"I was found by them that did not seek Me; I was manifested to those who did not ask for Me"** (Isaiah 65:1).

21 As to Israel He says, **"All the day long I spread out My hands to a disobedient and faultfinding people"** (Isaiah 65:2).

How Israel Stumbled

Romans 10:1-3: Israel stumbled the same way that many Christians now do—they tried to attain their standing with God through works. They failed to see how their righteousness must be based on the work of Christ. Good works have their place when done in faith and love. However, when we use them as a basis for establishing our standing before God, they are an affront to the cross of Jesus. His cross is the only way that we can be reconciled and stand righteously before God.

Paul explained that Israel had zeal for God, but not according to knowledge. Zeal that is self-centered and seeking self-righteousness can seem great. It can appear righteous and full of great love for God. Yet Paul himself is one of the great examples of this before his own conversion. Zeal based on works will lead you into direct conflict with the grace of God. This kind of zeal caused Paul to persecute true believers before his own discovery of grace by faith.

Christ is Salvation

10:4-11: True faith must come from the heart, not just the mind. You can understand a doctrine accurately and agree with it, but if it is not in your heart so that you live it, then it does not result in righteousness (v.10).

Unity in Christ

10:12-21: It is often said that we should preach the gospel in all things, and if necessary, use words. This sounds wise but, as we are told in verse fourteen, words are necessary for the preaching of the gospel. People will not be drawn to the grace of God by our good works, but will be drawn to us. The works of Christ done through us, such as miracles of healing, prophecy, etc., point to the power of the One we serve. After forty years of being in Christ, I have yet to hear the testimony of someone who was led to Christ by observing a Christian's good works. Those who come to Christ come by the witness and conviction of the Holy Spirit. We do good works because it is the right thing to do and because we love God and want to do what pleases Him. However, there must be a preacher for the anointed word to ignite faith in the heart.

NOTES:

PAUL'S LETTER TO THE
ROMANS
Romans 11

God's Faithfulness to Israel

1   Did God cast away His people? God forbid! I too am an Israelite, of the seed of Abraham, of the tribe of Benjamin.

2   God did not cast away His people whom He foreknew. Or do you not know what the Scripture says about Elijah? How he pleaded with God against Israel:

3   **"Lord, they have killed your prophets, they have torn down Your altars; and I alone am left, and they seek my life"** (I Kings 19:10).

4   What does God say in answer to him? **"I have left for Myself seven thousand men who have not bowed the knee to Baal"** (I Kings 19:18).

5   Just as then, at this present time there is also a remnant according to the election of grace.

6   However, if it is by grace, it is no longer by works, otherwise grace is not grace.

Israel Hardened

7   What shall we conclude? That which Israel sought for they did not obtain, but the elect obtained it, and the rest were hardened:

8   just as it is written, **"God gave them a spirit of stupor, eyes that they should not see, and ears that they should not hear, to this very day"** (see Deuteronomy 29:4; Isaiah 29:10).

9   And David said, **"Let their table be made a snare, and a trap, and a stumbling block, a just retribution to them.**

10 **"Let their eyes be darkened, that they may not see, and make their backs bow down always" (Psalm 69:22-23).**

11 I say then, did they stumble that they might fall? God forbid! By their fall salvation has come to the Gentiles, to provoke them to jealousy.

12 Now if their fall resulted in riches for the world, and their loss the riches of the Gentiles, how much more will their reinstatement mean?

13 As I speak to you that are Gentiles, as I am an apostle to the Gentiles, I glorify my ministry,

14 so that if by any means I may provoke to jealousy those that are my flesh and blood kinsman, and may save some of them.

15 For if their having been cut off has resulted in the reconciliation of the world, what will the receiving of them be but life from the dead?

16 If the firstfruit is holy, so is the lump, and if the root is holy, so are the branches.

Honoring our Roots

17 If some of the branches were broken off, and you, being a wild olive was grafted in among them, and did become a partaker with them of the root, and the fatness of the olive tree,

18 do not become arrogant toward the branches. If you glory, remember that it is not you that bears the root, but the root bears you.

19 You should say then, "Branches were broken off, that I might be grafted in."

20 By their unbelief they were broken off, and you stand by your faith. Do not be arrogant, but fear,

21 because if God did not spare the natural branches, neither will He spare you.

22 We must behold the kindness and the severity of God. Toward those who fell it is severity, but toward you, God's kindness, if you continue in His goodness, otherwise you also will be cut off.

23 They also, if they do not continue in their unbelief, will be grafted in, for God is able to graft them in again.

24 For if you were cut out of that which is by nature a wild olive tree, and were grafted contrary to nature into a good olive tree, how much more will these, which are the natural branches, be grafted into their own olive tree?

All Israel Will Be Saved

25 For I would not have you ignorant of this mystery, brethren, lest you become wise in your own conceits, that a partial hardening has taken place with Israel until the fullness of the Gentiles has come in.

26 So all Israel will be saved, even as it is written, **"There will come out of Zion the Deliverer; He will turn away ungodliness from Jacob"** (see Isaiah 59:20-21).

27 **"This is My covenant with them, when I will take away their sins"** (see Isaiah 27:9; Jeremiah 31:33).

28 From the perspective of the gospel they are enemies for your sake, but in regard to election, they are beloved for the sake of the fathers.

The Grace and the Mercy of God

29 For the gifts and the callings of God are irrevocable.

30 For just as you were disobedient to God in times past, but now have obtained mercy by their disobedience,

31 even so, they have also now been disobedient, that by the mercy shown to you they also may now obtain mercy.

32 For God has shut up all under disobedience so that He might have mercy upon all.

33 O the depth of the riches, and wisdom, and the knowledge of God! How unsearchable are His judgments, and His ways beyond discovery!

34 For who has known the mind of the Lord? Or who has been His counselor?

35 Or who has first given to Him, that He should owe them a debt?

36 For of Him, and through Him, and to Him, are all things. To Him be the glory for ever. Amen.

God's Faithfulness to Israel

Romans 11:1-6: The Book of Romans is considered the clearest deposition on New Covenant theology. It is especially clear in the explanation of the difference between law and grace. The contention between these was borne out in the conflict between the Jews, who still pursued a righteousness based on keeping the law, and the church, which was now being granted righteousness by their faith in Christ's atonement—grace.

Another related theme addressed here in this great epistle is that even though Paul writes of the Jew according to the spirit—the heart—God has not cast off His people whom He foreknew. Those who are Jews according to the flesh will continue to be a part of His ultimate purpose, which they will surely be grafted back into. This remains a controversy in the church to this day, but understanding this is vital to understanding God's ultimate purpose on earth.

As we see in Isaiah 11 and other prophecies, God's kingdom includes the restoration of the earth to the paradise it was originally created to be. We are seeking a heavenly inheritance, and yet we will rule and reign with Christ on earth for a thousand years. There will be an ultimate bridge and harmony between the heavens and the earth, just as the natural and spiritual seed will ultimately be joined in one purpose in Christ.

An important factor we must keep in mind as the two seeds, the spiritual and natural, come together is that this can only come through Christ. It will not be a joining of the law to grace as some suppose. The law was given as a tutor to lead us to Christ. However, once we come to Christ, if we continue to pursue righteousness by the law, we are rejecting the atonement of the cross through which mankind and the earth were redeemed.

Israel Hardened

11:7-16: When the Jews rejected their Messiah, it opened the door of faith to the Gentiles which began the time of the Gentiles. There had been about two thousand years from the time of Moses in which the Lord had dealt almost exclusively with the Jews in His unfolding plan of redeeming and restoring man and man's place of dominion, the earth. Paul was writing this epistle near the beginning of the two thousand years in which He would work through the Gentiles. At the end of this "time of the Gentiles," we see that the Jewish people will be grafted back into the tree. However, as Paul explains in Ephesians 2, what comes next is not another time of the Jews, but the time of the Jews and Gentiles together as "one new man."

In this text, we are also given the timing for the resurrection—when the Jews are grafted back in. This will be one of the great signs of the end of this age and the coming of the kingdom.

Honoring our Roots

11:17-24: The basic message of this passage is that arrogance will cut us off from the purposes of God. Therefore, Paul especially warns about becoming arrogant toward the natural branches—the Jewish people. Regardless of how hardened toward the gospel they remain, Jews are deserving of our honor for being the custodians of the Word of God, for being the womb that our Messiah came from, and for being the Lord's brethren according to the flesh.

We are also exhorted to "behold the kindness and the severity of God." Many can only see His kindness, and others can only see His severity, but to see Him as He is, we must be able to see both.

All Israel Will Be Saved

11:25-28: Paul states that for a time the Jews who are according to the flesh will be "enemies of the gospel," but this is "for our sake." Some of the greatest opposition to the gospel from the first century on has come from Jewish people, but it is for our sake. It helps us in this way: the Jewish people have been "hardened," or made hard to reach, in order to be the "acid test" that determines whether or not we have a faith that can penetrate this hardness and make them jealous for God again. Until our life and our message make Jews jealous, and help to soften their hearts to the gospel, we are not yet walking in the love and power that we are called to walk in.

The Jews were the most vehement persecutors of the young church, and now for centuries the church has persecuted Jewish people. This makes it more difficult for them to be open to the gospel, seeing it as a threat to their existence. However, until we have a message and an anointing that can break through this difficulty, we are not yet what we should be. Jewish people are the great test of our message. Until our message makes them jealous, we are not yet complete in our purpose.

Paul concludes this with the fact that Jews are beloved of God for the sake of the fathers. If we love God, then we will love whom He loves. There should be a special love for Jewish people in those who are united with Christ. However, true love requires us to never compromise the gospel or the need of Jewish people for their Messiah. There is no other way for them to be reconciled to God except by the provision He made through His Son.

The Grace and the Mercy of God

11:29-36: The Jewish people did both good and evil during the time of their custodianship of the purposes of God. We can now look back and say the same about the Gentiles during the church age. Both did some things well but have generally failed. The grace of God is about mercy for our failures, and we all need His mercy to come into His full purpose.

NOTES:

Paul's Letter To The
ROMANS
Romans 12

Transformation

1 I beseech you therefore, my brethren, by the mercies of God, to present your bodies a living sacrifice, holy, acceptable to God, which is your spiritual service.

2 Do not be conformed to this world, but be transformed by the renewing of your mind, so that you may prove what the will of God is; that which is good, acceptable, and perfect.

Being Joined to Him

3 For I say, through the grace that was given to me, to every man that is among you, not to think more highly of himself than he should, but to be of sober and sound judgment, just as God has dealt to each man a measure of faith.

4 For even as we have many members in one body, and all the members do not have the same function,

5 yet we who are many are one body in Christ, and are all members of one another.

6 We have gifts that differ according to the grace that was given to us. If we have the gift of prophecy, let us prophesy according to the proportion of our faith.

7 If we have the gift of service, let us give ourselves to this. If we are one who teaches, let us be devoted to that.

8 Let the one who exhorts be devoted to his exhorting. The one who gives should do it with liberality; the one who rules should do it with diligence; the one who shows mercy should do it with cheerfulness.

9   Let love be without hypocrisy. Abhor that which is evil; cleave to that which is good.

10 With love of the brethren be tenderly affectionate to one another, in honor preferring one another.

11 In diligence, not being slothful, but fervent in spirit; serving the Lord.

12 Rejoice in hope, be patient in tribulation, continuing steadfastly in prayer,

13 contributing to the needs of the saints, and devoted to hospitality.

14 Bless those who persecute you. Bless them and do not curse them in return.

Sowing Grace

15 Rejoice with those who rejoice; weep with those who weep.

16 Be of the same mind toward one another. Do not just mind those who are prominent, but also consider the lowly. Do not be wise in your own eyes.

17 Do not return evil for evil. Be considerate of the things that are honorable in the sight of all men.

18 If it is possible, as much as it depends on you, be at peace with all men.

19 Do not avenge yourselves, beloved, but give opportunity for the wrath of God, for it is written, **"Vengeance belongs to Me; I will recompense evil," says the Lord (see Deuteronomy 32:35).**

20 If your enemy is hungry, feed him. If he is thirsty, give him a drink. In doing this you shall heap coals of fire upon his head.

21 Do not be overcome with evil, but overcome evil with good.

Transformation

Romans 12:1-2: This is the basic path to being transformed into the image of Christ. It begins with the understanding that we were bought with a price, and we no longer belong to ourselves but to Christ. True Christianity is a life of sacrifice, yet to be His slave is the most freedom we can ever experience. When we give our lives to Him, we find life.

Maturity in Christ means we will no longer think like the world, or be like it. We are citizens of another nation, a holy nation, which is another reality. If we are still thinking the way the world does, and our thoughts are dominated by the things of this world, then we have not yet had our minds transformed.

When our minds have been transformed, we will be able to prove what the will of God is and will walk in the greatest confidence and peace that can be known on this earth.

Being Joined to Him

12:3-14: We cannot be properly joined to the Head without also being joined to His body. Being joined to Christ means that we are a functioning member of His body—knowing and doing our part to build up the whole body. Every Christian has a ministry. Every Christian has been given gifts of the Spirit that are tools used to fulfill their purpose. Those who are growing up in Christ are growing in their own purpose, too.

As we grow in our place in His body, our affection for the whole body will grow. Loving and serving others is one of the great joys of life, and the body of Christ should be the ultimate example of this. As we do unto even the least of His little ones, we are doing to Him. How would you like to take Jesus out to dinner tonight? You can do that by taking one of His people.

Sowing Grace

12:15-21: This is the exhortation to true Christian behavior which, when followed, prospers the soul and leads to the greatest peace and joy. As we are told in Galatians, we will reap what we sow. If we want to reap grace, we must learn to sow grace every chance we get. If we want to reap mercy, we must sow mercy every chance we get. This is the nature of the Christian life. Like Christ, we are to go around doing good.

NOTES:

PAUL'S LETTER TO THE
ROMANS
Romans 13

Authority

1   Let every one be in subjection to those in authority, for there is no authority except from God, and those that exist are ordained by God.

2   Therefore the one who opposes authority opposes the ordinance of God, and those who oppose will receive judgment upon themselves.

3   For rulers are not to be feared by those who do good but by those who do evil. If you want to have no fear of authority, do what is right, and you will have praise from the same.

4   It is a minister of God to you for good. If you do what is evil, be afraid, for it does not bear the sword for nothing, but is a minister of God to avenge evil and bring wrath on the one that does evil.

5   Therefore you must be in subjection to authority, not only because of wrath, but also for the sake of your conscience.

6   For this cause you also pay taxes, for they are ministers in God's service, attending continually to this very thing.

7   Render to all that which is due them: taxes to whom taxes are due, custom to whom custom, respect to whom respect, honor to whom honor.

Fulfilling the Law

8   Do not be under obligation to anyone, except to love one another, because he that loves his neighbor has fulfilled the law.

9   For it is written, **"You shall not commit adultery, You shall not kill, You shall not steal, You shall not covet"** (see Exodus 20:13-17),

and if there is any other commandment, it is summed up in this word, namely, **"You shall love your neighbor as yourself"** (see Leviticus 19:18).

10 Love does not do wrong to his neighbor. Love is therefore the fulfillment of the law.

11 Know the times, that already it is time for you to awaken out of your sleep, for now our salvation is nearer to us than when we first believed.

12 The night is gone, and the day is at hand. Let us therefore cast off the works of darkness, and let us put on the armor of light.

13 Let us walk uprightly, as in the day, not in reveling and drunkenness, not in lewdness and lust, not in strife or jealousy.

14 Put on the Lord Jesus Christ, and do not make any provision for the flesh and its lusts.

Authority

Romans 13:1-7: This is a difficult text for many to understand. Does this mean that Hitler and Stalin were appointed by God? No. As we see in the Book of Acts, when the apostles were told not to preach in the name of Jesus anymore, the very thing Jesus had commissioned them to do, they said that they must obey God rather than men. When human, civil authority directly conflicts with the will of God, then we are to obey God.

This text could have read that there is no authority except that which is allowed by God. We need to consider that when Paul was writing this, Nero, one of the most wicked of all the Caesars, and the very one who would take Paul's own life, was the emperor. So this does not mean that we disobey authority just because it is evil, but we refuse to obey only those commands that are in direct conflict with God's commandments.

All authority is allowed by God, including Hitler, Stalin, and every other evil despot. This does not mean that they are God's will, but as we are told in Psalm 115:16, "The heavens are the heavens of the Lord, but the earth He has given to the sons of men." This is why He will not do things on earth without us asking Him. He delegated the authority over the earth to man, and man chose to follow the devil. All evil in the world is the result of that choice and the continued choice of man to follow evil instead of turning to God. Therefore, the evil despots are man's choice and the consequences of not obeying God. God does not want this, but He has to allow it. There can be no true obedience if there is not the freedom to disobey, but disobedience does have consequences.

As we see in the first five chapters of Isaiah and other places in Scripture, wicked, immature, or capricious rulers are a judgment of God against nations who fall to wickedness. The wickedness described by Isaiah is to start calling good evil and evil good, to honor the dishonorable, and to dishonor the honorable. This is precisely what has happened to Western civilization in recent times and is the reason why we have also been afflicted with increasingly wicked, immature, and capricious leadership.

Fulfilling the law

13:8-14: The antidote to the corruption of the flesh is to live by the Spirit, which can be summed up by love. If we walk in love, we fulfill the law. If we love God, we will not worship idols. If we love others, we will not steal from them, murder them, or do them any wrong; so in this way love fulfills the law.

NOTES:

PAUL'S LETTER TO THE
ROMANS
Romans 14

Using Liberty to Love

1   Receive the one who is weak, and not for judging them.

2   One may have faith to eat all things, but another who is weak eats vegetables only.

3   Let not the one who eats judge the one who does not eat. Let not the one who does not eat judge the one who eats, for God has received him.

4   Who are you to judge the servant of another? To their own Lord they will stand or fall. Yes, they can be made to stand, because the Lord has the power to make them stand.

5   One esteems one day above another. Another esteems every day alike. Let each one be fully convinced in his own mind about such matters.

6   The one who regards the day regards it to the Lord, and the one who eats, eats as unto the Lord, for they give God thanks. The one who does not eat does not eat as unto the Lord, and likewise gives God thanks.

7   For none of us lives to himself, and none dies to himself.

8   For if we live, we live for the Lord, or if we die, we die for the Lord. Whether we live therefore, or die, we are the Lord's.

9   It was to this end Christ died and rose again, that He might be Lord of both the dead and the living.

10 So why do you judge your brother? Or why do you show contempt for your brother? We will all stand before the judgment seat of God,

11 because it is written, **"As I live, says the Lord, to Me every knee shall bow, and every tongue shall confess God" (Isaiah 45:23).**

12 So then each one of us will give account of himself to God.

13 Let us therefore not judge one another anymore, but rather determine this, that no man puts a stumbling block in his brother's way, or give him an occasion to fall.

14 I know, and am persuaded in the Lord Jesus, that nothing is unclean of itself, unless one considers it to be unclean, then to him it is unclean.

15 Therefore, if because of food your brother is offended, you are no longer walking in love. Do not let what you eat harm the one for whom Christ died.

16 Do not let your good be spoken of as evil because of this.

17 The kingdom of God is not eating and drinking, but righteousness, peace, and joy in the Holy Spirit.

18 He that in this way serves Christ is well-pleasing to God, and finds approval with men.

19 So then let us follow after the things that make for peace, and things that edify one another.

20 Do not tear down the work of God for the sake of food. All things indeed are clean, but it is evil for that man who eats with a guilty conscience.

21 It is good not to eat foods, nor to drink wine, nor to do anything that would cause a brother to stumble.

22 The faith that you have, have to yourself before God. Happy is the one that does not condemn himself in that which he approves.

23 He that doubts is condemned if he eats, because he does not eat in faith, and whatever is not of faith is sin.

Using Liberty to Love

Romans 14:1-23: One of the biggest battles that all who seek to walk righteously before the Lord have is to fight self-righteousness. When you are fasting or doing something special to seek the Lord, have you ever wondered why you are tempted to start looking critically at those who are not making the same kind of sacrifice that you are? That is the beginning

of self-righteousness, and it is repelling to both God and man. This is why Paul combined both the exhortation to not judge others and the liberty we are given to hold differing opinions about the non-essentials.

The New Testament is not meant to be another law. It is not meant to be such a strict master that we cannot do anything that is not written in it; rather, it is meant to free us to do whatever is not specifically forbidden by it. This does not mean that what we choose to do is right, but that we must each seek the guidance of the Holy Spirit and always walk by the higher law of love. Though we may have the freedom to do something, it does not make it right. There are times when love should constrain us. The Lord did not want us to live under commandments, but under love.

NOTES:

Paul's Letter To The
ROMANS
Romans 15

Christian Service in Unity

1   Now we who are strong should bear the weaknesses of those who are weak, and not just please ourselves.

2   Let each one of us please his neighbor in what is good and for edification.

3   For Christ did not please Himself; but as it is written, **"The reproaches of them that reproached you fell upon Me" (Psalm 69:9).**

4   Everything that was written before was written for our instruction, that through patience, and through the comfort of the Scriptures, we might have hope.

5   Now may the God of patience and comfort grant you to be of the same mind with one another according to Christ Jesus,

6   so that with one accord you may with one mouth glorify the God and Father of our Lord Jesus Christ.

7   Therefore receive one another, even as Christ also received you, to the glory of God.

Hope for Jews and Gentiles

8   Christ has been made a minister of the circumcision for the truth of God, so that He might confirm the promises given to the fathers,

9   and so that the Gentiles might glorify God for His mercy; as it is written, **"Therefore will I give praise to You among the Gentiles, and sing to Your name" (Psalm 18:49).**

10 Again he says, **"Rejoice, you Gentiles, with His people" (Deuteronomy 32: 43).**

11 And, **"Praise the Lord, all of you Gentiles; and let all the peoples praise Him"** (Psalm 117:1).

12 Yet again, Isaiah says, **"There shall come from the root of Jesse, He that arises to rule over the Gentiles. On Him will the Gentiles hope"** (see Isaiah 11:1,10; Revelation 22:16).

13 Now, may the God of hope fill you with all joy and peace in believing, that you may abound in hope, in the power of the Holy Spirit.

14 I am persuaded that you, my brethren, are full of goodness, filled with knowledge, able also to admonish one another.

15 I write boldly to you in some measure, to bring to your remembrance these things, because of the grace that was given to me by God,

16 that I should be a minister of Christ Jesus to the Gentiles, serving the gospel of God, that the offering of the Gentiles might be made acceptable, being sanctified by the Holy Spirit.

Preaching the Gospel with Power

17 I have therefore my own glorifying in Christ Jesus in things pertaining to God.

18 For I will not dare to speak of anything except those things that Christ has wrought through me, for the obedience of the Gentiles, by word and deed,

19 in the power of signs and wonders, in the power of the Holy Spirit, so that from Jerusalem, and round about even to Illyricum, I have preached the full gospel of Christ.

20 Yes, I made it my goal not to preach the gospel where Christ was already preached, so that I would not build upon another man's foundation;

21 but, as it is written, **"They shall see, to whom no news of Him came, and those who have not heard shall understand"** (Isaiah 52:15).

22 Therefore, I have been hindered many times from coming to you,

23 but now, not having any other place in these regions to preach, and having had for many years a longing to come to you,

24 when I go to Spain I hope to see you on my journey, and to be helped on my way by you, after I have been strengthened by your company.

The Gentiles Help Their Jewish Brethren

25 However, now I will go to Jerusalem, as a ministry to the saints.

26 For it has been the good pleasure of Macedonia and Achaia to make a noteworthy contribution for the poor among the saints that are at Jerusalem.

27 Yes, it has been their good pleasure as they are their debtors. For if the Gentiles have been made partakers of their spiritual things, they owe it to them also to minister to them in natural things.

28 When therefore I have accomplished this, and have sealed this fruit, I will go on my way by you to Spain.

29 I know that when I come to you, I will come in the fullness of the blessing of Christ.

30 Now I beseech you, brethren, by our Lord Jesus Christ, and by the love of the Spirit, that you strive together with me in your prayers to God for me,

31 so that I may be delivered from those who are disobedient in Judea, and that my service for the saints in Jerusalem may be acceptable to them,

32 so that I may then come to you in joy in the will of God, and together with you find rest.

33 Now the God of peace be with you all. Amen.

Christian Service in Unity

Romans 15:1-7: The conclusion of all of Paul's theology is summed up by how we must love and care for one another for the sake of Christ Jesus.

Hope for Jews and Gentiles

15:8-16: Paul had a basic mission to not only reach the Gentiles for Christ, but to help them understand their place in God's plan and their relationship to their Jewish brethren in Christ. A key to the unity we are called to is that in all things we are to keep our hope in God and His salvation, whose perfect plan was so clearly foretold and has so perfectly unfolded.

Preaching the Gospel with Power

15:17-24: One of the emerging great Gentile churches in the world, the church in Rome, was begun without Paul, "the apostle to the Gentiles." Even so, Paul very much desired to have a part in its growth and fruit. At the time of this writing, he obviously did not yet know that he would spend the last two years of his life in Rome. It was to Rome that Paul wrote one of his greatest epistles, and it was from Rome that he would write some of his others. Paul's epistles would be included together with the most powerful words ever written—the Scriptures. After nearly two thousand years, they are still impacting the world like nothing else.

The Gentiles Help Their Jewish Brethren

15:25-33: Paul considered it an important mission to carry gifts from the Gentiles to their Jewish brethren. By this, he was building a bridge of trust between the Jews and their new Gentile brethren that was necessary to help both.

NOTES:

PAUL'S LETTER TO THE
ROMANS
Romans 16

Recommendation of Fellow Workers

1 I commend to you Phoebe our sister, who is a servant of the church that is at Cenchreae:

2 that you receive her in the Lord, in a manner worthy of the saints, and that you assist her in what matters she may have need of from you, because she herself has been a helper of many, as well as to me.

3 Salute Priscilla and Aquila my fellow-workers in Christ Jesus,

4 who for my life risked their own necks; to whom I owe much, as also do all the churches of the Gentiles.

5 Salute the church that is in their house. Salute Epaenetus my beloved, who is the first-fruits of Asia to Christ.

6 Salute Mary, who labored much for you.

7 Salute Andronicus and Junias, my kinsmen, and my fellow-prisoners, who are of note among the apostles, who were also in Christ before me.

8 Salute Ampliatus my beloved in the Lord.

9 Salute Urbanus our fellow-worker in Christ, and Stachys my beloved.

10 Salute Apelles the approved in Christ. Salute those who are of the household of Aristobulus.

11 Salute Herodion my kinsman. Salute those who are of the household of Narcissus that are in the Lord.

12 Salute Tryphaena and Tryphosa, who labor in the Lord. Salute Persis the beloved, who labored much in the Lord.

13 Salute Rufus the chosen in the Lord, and his mother and mine.

14 Salute Asyncritus, Phlegon, Hermes, Patrobas, Hermas, and the brethren that are with them.

15 Salute Philologus and Julia, Nereus and his sister, and Olympas, and all the saints that are with them.

16 Salute one another with a holy kiss. All the churches of Christ salute you.

Those Who Cause Divisions

17 Now I beseech you, brethren, mark those who are causing divisions and occasions for stumbling that are contrary to the doctrine that you have learned, and turn away from them.

18 For they that are this way do not serve our Lord Jesus Christ, but their own appetite. By their smooth and fair speech they beguile the hearts of the innocent.

19 For your obedience has been made known abroad to all men. I rejoice therefore over you. Even so, I would have you wise in that which is good, but simple concerning that which is evil.

The God of Peace

20 The God of peace will soon crush Satan under your feet. The grace of our Lord Jesus Christ be with you.

21 Timothy my fellow-worker salutes you, as well as Lucius, Jason and Sosipater, my kinsmen.

22 Tertius, who wrote this letter for me, salutes you in the Lord.

23 Gaius my host, and the whole church, salutes you. Erastus the treasurer of the city salutes you, and Quartus the brother.

24 May the grace of our Lord Jesus Christ be with you all. Amen.

25 Now to Him who is able to establish you according to my gospel, and the preaching of Jesus Christ, according to the revelation of the mystery which has been kept in silence through times eternal,

26 but now is manifested, and by the Scriptures of the prophets, according to the commandment of the eternal God, is made known to all the nations leading to the obedience of faith,

27 to the only wise God, through Jesus Christ, to whom be the glory forever. Amen.

Recommendation of Fellow Workers

Romans 16:1-16: Paul was always intent on acknowledging the work of others and recommending them and their work to the churches. His letters of recommendation later became the basis for college degrees. Just as his recommendations were only as good as his own reputation, the same is still true of a college degree. The value of the degree is determined by the reputation of the institution issuing it. In our time, endorsements by well-known people have reached unprecedented use. Even so, endorsements have been cheapened. They started to lose their value because they could be purchased, and because it was discovered that many who endorsed products were not even using them. What would our recommendation be worth? Not just in money, but in influence? Have we kept the integrity of our name so that it still has value?

In one of the greatest of all wonders, the One with the greatest and most valuable name of all—Jesus—has given us the authority to use His name! Let us keep this unfathomable honor with the greatest of care so that it is always esteemed with the value it deserves.

Those Who Cause Divisions

16:17-19: One can have charisma and teachings that seem good, but if the fruit causes division, there is poison mixed in. It is a basic responsibility of the leaders of the church to "mark" those in order to protect the ones given into their charge and to warn others about them.

The God of Peace

16:20-27: The Lord uses the title "Lord of hosts," or "Lord of armies," over ten times more than all His other titles. He is a marshal God, a military leader, yet it is the "God of peace" who will crush Satan under our feet. The peace of God is one of the most powerful of the "divinely powerful weapons" we have been given. When we abide in the peace of God, we are abiding in an impregnable fortress. When we walk and live in the peace of God, we will expose and cast out darkness with this great light, especially in these times of increasing fear and chaos. Never lose the peace of God, and the God of peace be with you.

NOTES:

Paul's Letter to the Romans Proper Names and Definitions

Abba: Dad or Papa

Abraham: father of a great multitude, exalted father

Achaia: grief, trouble

Adam: man, red, earth

Andronicus: a man excelling others

Apelles: exclusion, separation

Aquila: an eagle

Aristobulus: a good counselor

Asia: muddy, boggy

Asyncritus: incomparable

Baal: master, Lord

Benjamin: son of the right hand

Christ: anointed

David: well-beloved, dear

Elijah: heifer, chariot, round, Yah is God

Erastus: lovely, amiable

Esau: hairy, rough, he that acts or finishes

Gaius: Lord, an earthly man

Gentiles: the nations or pagan

Gomorrah: rebellious people, submersion, to deal tyrannically; make merchandise of; a ruined heap

Hermas: Hermes, Mercury, gain, refuge

Hermes: Mercury, gain, refuge

Herodion: the song of Juno

Hosea: Hoshea, savior, safety, deliverer

Illyricum: joy, rejoicing

Isaac: laughter, he shall laugh, mockery

Isaiah: the salvation of the LORD

Israel: who prevails with God, he shall be prince of God

Israelite: prince with God

Israelites: descendants of Israel, prevails with God

Jacob: that supplants, undermines, heel-catcher

Jason: he that cures

Jerusalem: vision of peace, foundation of peace, restoring or teaching of peace

Jesse: gift, oblation, one who is, possessor, wealthy, Yahweh exists, man, manly, strong

Jesus: Savior, Deliverer, Yahweh is salvation

Jew: the praise of the LORD, confession

Joel: he that wills or commands, Jehovah is God

Julia: downy, soft and tender hair

Macedonia: burning, adoration

Mark: polite, shining

Mary: bitterness, rebellion

Moses: taken out, drawn forth

Narcissus: astonishment, stupidity

Nereus: a lamp, new-tilled land

Olympas: heavenly

Patrobas: paternal, that pursues the steps of his father

Paul: small, little

Persis: that cuts or divides, a nail, a gryphon, a horseman

Pharaoh: that disperses, that spoils, great house, his nakedness

Philologus: a lover of letters, or of the word

Phlegon: zealous, burning

Priscilla: ancient

Quartus: fourth

Rome: strength, power

Rufus: red

Sabaoth: Lord of hosts

Sarah: lady, princess, princess of the multitude, have dominion

Satan: contrary, adversary, enemy, accuser, deceiver

Sodom: their secret, their cement, fettered, scorch, burnt

Spain: rare, precious

Stachys: spike or ear of corn

Tertius: third

Tryphosa: thrice shining

Zion: monument, raised up, sepulcher, fortification, permanent capital, barren, dry, desert

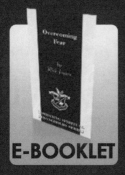

NOW FEATURING WORK EDUCATIONAL PROGRAM
MorningStar University
SCHOOL OF THEOLOGY AND DOCTRINE
SCHOOL OF THE HOLY SPIRIT
SCHOOL OF MISSIONS
RELEASING A SUPERNATURAL ARMY TO TRANSFORM THE WORLD
BUILD STRONG BIBLICAL FOUNDATIONS AND A CHRISTIAN WORLDVIEW
GAIN PRACTICAL AND SUPERNATURAL TOOLS FOR SUCCESS
ENGAGE IN "SPECIAL FORCES" MISSION OPPORTUNITIES
INTERN WITH INTERNATIONAL MINISTRY, EDUCATION, AND BUSINESS LEADERS
1, 2, AND 3 YEAR PROGRAMS AVAILABLE
* ASSOCIATE DEGREES AVAILABLE
NOW ACCEPTING APPLICATIONS
FIND YOUR DESTINY
IMPACT HISTORY
CHANGE THE WORLD
FOR MORE INFORMATION
CALL: 803-802-5544, EXTENSION 238
VISIT: WWW.MORNINGSTARUNIVERSITY.COM
EMAIL: MSUOFFICE@MORNINGSTARMINISTRIES.ORG